D0707508

Finger Rhymes

Compiled by John Foster

Illustrated by Carol Thompson

Oxford University Press

Oxford   New York   Toronto

Oxford University Press, Great Clarendon Street, Oxford OX2 6DP

Oxford   New York
Athens   Auckland   Bangkok   Bogota   Bombay
Buenos Aires   Calcutta   Cape Town   Dar es Salaam
Delhi   Florence   Hong Kong   Istanbul   Karachi
Kuala Lumpur   Madras   Madrid   Melbourne
Mexico City   Nairobi   Paris   Singapore
Taipei   Tokyo   Toronto

and associated companies in
Berlin   Ibadan

Oxford is a trade mark of Oxford University Press

This selection and arrangement © John Foster 1996
Illustrations © Carol Thompson 1996
First published 1996
Reprinted 1997

John Foster and Carol Thompson have asserted their moral
right to be identified as the authors of this work

All rights reserved. No part of this publication may be
reproduced, stored in a retrieval system, or transmitted, in
any form or by any means, without the prior
permission in writing of Oxford University Press.
Within the U.K., exceptions are allowed in respect of
any fair dealing for the purpose of research or private
study, or criticism or review, as permitted under the
Copyright, Designs and Patents Act, 1988, or in the
case of reprographic reproduction in accordance
with the terms of the licences issued by the
Copyright Licensing Agency.
Enquiries concerning reproduction outside these terms
and in other countries should be sent to
the Rights Department, Oxford University Press,
at the address above.

A CIP catalogue record for this book is available
from the British Library

ISBN 0 19 276142 0

Printed in Belgium

Contents

Five Little Fingers

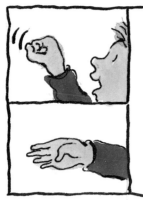

Five little fingers
Knocking on a door;
One slipped through the letter-box,
Then there were four.

Four little fingers
Climbing up a tree;
One forgot to hold on tight,
Then there were three.

Three little fingers
Eating Irish stew;
One fell in the stew pot,
Then there were two.

Two little fingers
Walking by a pond;
One slipped in the water,
Then there was one.

One little finger
Sleeping on the floor;
Woke up in the morning
And found the other four.

Jack Ousbey

Finger Play

One finger
Two fingers
Three fingers
Four,
One, two, three, four,
What are fingers for?
Pointing fingers
Crossing fingers
Grabbing fingers, too,

Stretching fingers
Hugging fingers
What else can they do?
Bending fingers
Hiding fingers
Need a thumb who's missed,
Thumb lays over
Hiding fingers –
Look!
I've made a fist!

Babs Bell Hajdusiewicz

This Finger's Straight

This finger's straight;
This finger's curled;
This one's the tallest
In the world;
This finger stands
At the end of the line;
Here's a fat thumb
And I think it's mine.

Jack Ousbey

12

Letter Shapes

Point with your finger.
Point to the sky.
If you put a dot on top
You can make a letter i.

Curve your thumb and finger.
Make a letter c.
It's shaped like a banana
You can eat for your tea.

Touch your thumb with your finger.
Make a letter o.
Put it round your lips
And blow, blow, blow!

John Foster

13

The Bird

Here are the legs
that walk along.

Here is the beak
that sings a song.

Here are the wings
that flap and spread.

mmm....
Squirmy, squirmy
worm!

And here is the bird
above my head.

Tony Mitton

Squirmy Earthworm

Squirmy, squirmy earthworm
Lives down in the ground.
But watch her wiggle out
When rain falls all around!

Squirmy, squirmy earthworm
Squirms along the ground.
But watch her disappear when
Blackbirds come around!

Babs Bell Hajdusiewicz

Foxy Down a Rabbit Hole

Foxy down a rabbit hole,
Looking for a bunny,
Bunny bit him on the nose,
OW! That wasn't funny!

Foxy down a mousie hole
Looking for some mice,
Mousie bit him on the nose,
OW! That wasn't nice!

Foxy down his own hole,
Lots of noisy sobbing,
Putting ointment on his nose
To try and stop it throbbing.

Kaye Umansky

Caterpillar

I can see a caterpillar
Wriggling on a leaf.

It wriggles on the top and
It wriggles underneath.

Then one day it's very still.

I stand quietly watching till
It changes shape and falls asleep.

18

Every day I take a peep.
Then at last, it moves about.

I'm so surprised, I give a shout.
For now there's a butterfly
Sitting on the leaf.

It spreads its wings
And flies about.

Delphine Evans

19

Seaside Song

Here are the cliffs.

Here are the seas.

Here are the waves
that rock in the breeze.

Here are the fishes
that dart and play.

And here are the seagulls
that fly away.

Tony Mitton

See These Fingers

See these fingers
See this hand,
Here's a crab
Walking on the sand;

Here it comes,
Watch it go,
Make sure it doesn't
Nip your toe.

Tony Langham

Look out!

Firework

Here is a sparkler.
Hold it with care.
Scribble with gold
in the cold night air.

Here are the flames
that flicker and burn.
See how they dance
as they twist and turn.

And here is a rocket
that races high.
See how it bursts
in the brilliant sky.

Tony Mitton

Here is a ring on a silver dish.

Put it on your finger and make a wish.

Here is a genie who waits in a flask.

If you want a favour whisper and ask.

If I Had a Silver Coin

If I had a silver coin,
I'd take it to the shop

And I would buy myself a lovel
Orange lollipop.

I'd unwrap all the paper

And I'd lick and lick and lick,

And when I'd finished licking
I'd only have the stick.

I wouldn't throw it on the ground,
I wouldn't poke my brother,

I'd put it in the rubbish bin –

I wish I had another.

Wendy Cope

Wheeeeee

The Slide

Up the steps we're climbing,
careful not to trip.

At the top
a little hop –
Wheeeeeeeee,
down we slip!

Tony Mitton

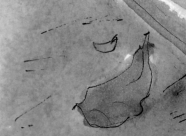

We are grateful for permission to include the following poems in this collection:

Wendy Cope: 'If I had a ten pence piece' (retitled 'If I Had a Silver Coin' with the author's agreement) from *Twiddling Your Thumbs: Hand Rhymes* by Wendy Cope, reprinted by permission of the publishers, Faber & Faber Ltd. **Delphine Evans:** 'Caterpillar' from *Fingers, Feet & Fun,* written and compiled by Delphine Evans (Hutchinson), reprinted by permission of Random House UK Ltd. **John Foster:** 'Letter Shapes' (first published with the title 'Point with your finger') from *Themes for Early Years: Shapes,* compiled by Irene Yates (Scholastic, 1995), Copyright © John Foster 1995, reprinted by permission of the author. **Babs Bell Hajdusiewicz:** 'Finger Play' and 'Squirmy Earthworm', first published in *Poetry Works! The First Verse,* collection © 1993 by Modern Curriculum Press, reprinted by permission of the author. **Tony Langham:** 'See These Fingers', Copyright © Tony Langham 1996, first published in this collection by permission of the author. **Tony Mitton:** 'The Bird', 'Seaside Song', 'Firework', 'Arabian Nights', and 'The Slide', Copyright © Tony Mitton 1996, first published in this collection by permission of the author. **Jack Ousbey:** 'Five Little Fingers' and 'This Finger's Straight', Copyright © Jack Ousbey 1996, first published in this collection by permission of the author. **Kaye Umansky:** 'Foxy Down a Rabbit Hole', Copyright © Kaye Umansky 1996, first published in this collection by permission of Caroline Sheldon Literary Agency and of the author.